MYG AND ME

A-myg-da-la ... Amygdala. But I just say Myg. I want to tell you about Myg. How Myg looks out for me, how Myg helps to keep me safe and why Myg is always there. And why sometimes Myg works too hard and I have to take charge!

This charming storybook introduces Myg the Amygdala within the context of 'my brilliant brain' – giving children usable knowledge to help them understand what happens when they feel worried or anxious.

Alongside vibrant and engaging illustrations, this book:

- Teaches children what anxiety is, where it comes from and why it happens.

- Provides easy to understand and relatable context so that children can correctly identify and anticipate their emotions, helping them to understand that they can be in control of their feelings, their thoughts and their actions.

- Shares simple strategies and encouragement for children to manage their anxiety and self-calm, teaching them that they do not have to be controlled and limited by their fears and anxieties.

- Communicates that everyone feels anxiety and it's OK to ask for help.

T0002789

Designed for use alongside the guidebook titled My Brilliant Brain: *A Practical Resource for Understanding Anxiety and Implementing Self-Calming*, this book will be an important tool for teachers, support staff, therapists and parents seeking to enhance children's resilience, wellbeing and emotional health development.

Liz Bates is an independent education consultant. She supports both primary and secondary schools in all aspects of Emotional Health and Wellbeing, and Safeguarding, including whole school approaches, training staff and delivering talks to parents. Liz is a Protective Behaviours Trainer, a Wellbeing Award Advisor for Optimus and a regular contributor at national conferences.

Myg and Me

Understanding Anxiety and Implementing Self-Calming

Liz Bates

Illustrated by Nigel Dodds

Routledge
Taylor & Francis Group

LONDON AND NEW YORK

First published 2022
by Routledge
2 Park Square, Milton Park, Abingdon, Oxon OX14 4RN

and by Routledge
605 Third Avenue, New York, NY 10158

Routledge is an imprint of the Taylor & Francis Group, an informa business

© 2022 Liz Bates and Nigel Dodds

The right of Liz Bates to be identified as author and Nigel Dodds to be identified as illustrator of this work has been asserted by them in accordance with sections 77 and 78 of the Copyright, Designs and Patents Act 1988.

All rights reserved. No part of this book may be reprinted or reproduced or utilised in any form or by any electronic, mechanical, or other means, now known or hereafter invented, including photocopying and recording, or in any information storage or retrieval system, without permission in writing from the publishers.

Trademark notice: Product or corporate names may be trademarks or registered trademarks, and are used only for identification and explanation without intent to infringe.

British Library Cataloguing-in-Publication Data
A catalogue record for this book is available from the British Library

Library of Congress Cataloging-in-Publication Data
A catalog record has been requested for this book

ISBN: 978-1-032-06910-4 (pbk)
ISBN: 978-1-003-20447-3 (ebk)

DOI: 10.4324/9781003204473

Typeset in Apple Casual
by codeMantra

My brain is brilliant.

And yours is, too.

We have brilliant brains.

This is to certify
my brain is

Brilliant!

My brain helps me ...

run, jump, sing, dance, make up stories,

work things out, learn new stuff ...

What else do you think your brain helps you to do?

1

If I want to remember a funny joke to tell my friends. My brilliant brain helps me to remember. What else do you think it helps me to remember?

If I need to concentrate hard on a game. My brilliant brain helps me to concentrate. What else do you think it helps me to concentrate on?

If I want to learn a new dance move. My brilliant brain helps me to learn. What else do you think it helps me to learn?

There is a very special part of my brain.

I call that part Myg.

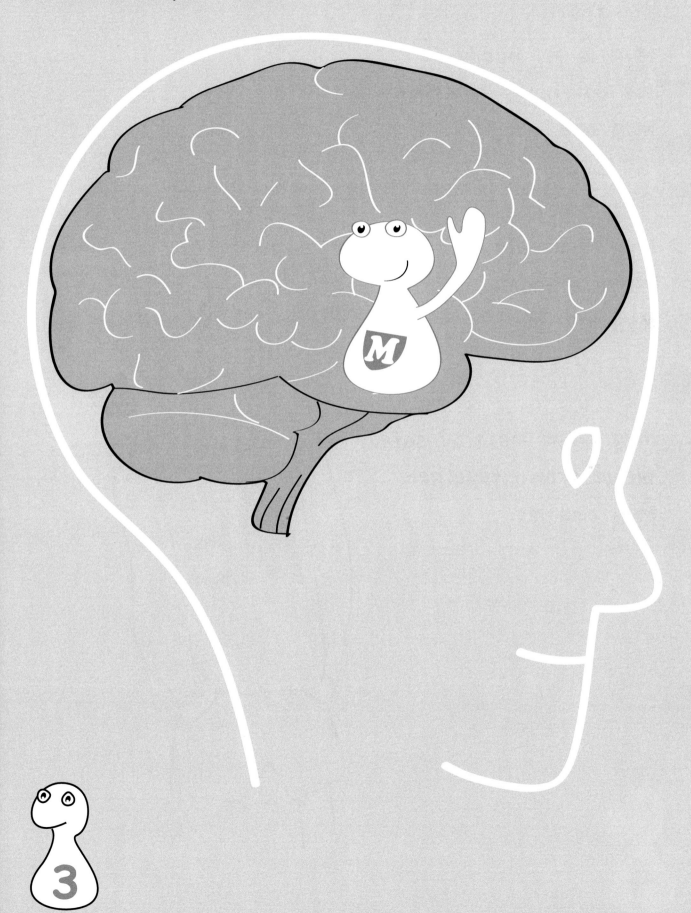

Myg is my buddy.
We do things together.
Myg and me.

Myg looks out for me.
We're a team.
Myg and me.

Myg helps me stay safe.
We've grown together.
Myg and me.

4

Myg is a nickname.

Myg's full name is long. Here we go ...

A-myg-da-la ... Amygdala.

But I just say Myg.

I want to tell you about Myg.

How Myg looks out for me, how Myg helps to keep me safe and why Myg is always there.

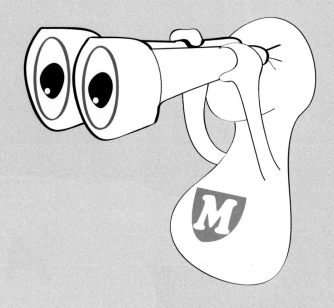

And why sometimes Myg works too hard and I have to take charge!

Myg is always there, because Myg is tucked away, deep in my brain.
Myg was there in my brain, even before I was born.

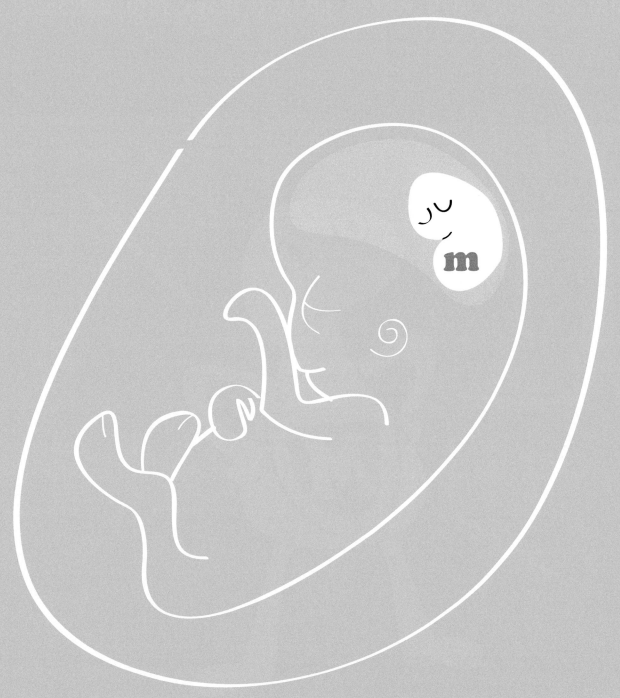

And you have a Myg, too.
Although you may use a different name.

Myg has been looking after me all of my life.
If I feel anxious, or worried, or scared, or nervous,
that is when Myg wakes up and leaps into action.

If I met an alien who wanted me to go in their spaceship, Myg would help me to shout 'No!!!' at the top of my voice and help me to throw my backpack at the alien to scare it off.

If I was in the garden and a crocodile wandered in, Myg would power up my legs to help me to run away really fast.

If a big, purple, hairy monster peered through my window, Myg would help me to stay really still, so it wouldn't see me and would fly on somewhere else.

11

Myg knows what to do, even before I do.
And I wouldn't want to be without Myg.

And your Myg is exactly the same.

Myg knows when there is trouble. This is how Myg looks out for me and keeps me safe.

Myg can send messages to my brain. And my brain sends messages to the rest of my body – so quickly that I don't know it is happening.

Myg gets my heart beating fast, to pump blood round my body.

Myg gets my breathing to speed up, to get more oxygen into my blood.

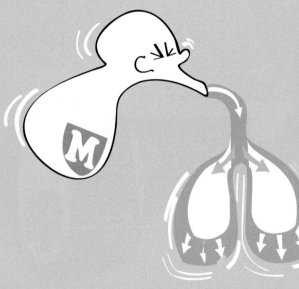

Myg shuts down my stomach, so that all my energy can go to my legs.

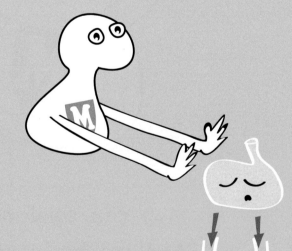

14

Yes, Myg knows exactly what to do.

But sometimes Myg works a bit too hard.

Sometimes, Myg doesn't know when to take a break.

Sometimes, I have to take charge.

15

If I am finding a school test really hard, Myg thinks I need help.
Just like with the alien, Myg wants me to shout 'No!' and tear up the test paper ... even if I want to have a go at the test!

If I am meeting my neighbour's new dog for the first time, Myg thinks I am not safe.
Just like with the crocodile Myg powers up my legs to run away really fast ... even if I want to meet the dog.

17

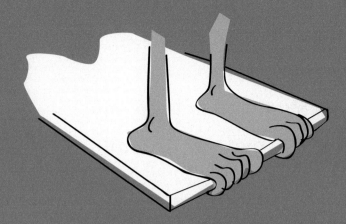

If I am standing on the diving board at the swimming pool, Myg thinks I am in danger.

Just like with a big, purple, hairy monster, Myg freezes my feet to the diving board to stop me from jumping off ... even when I want to!

Myg thinks I need protecting, sometimes when I don't. This is because Myg can't always tell the difference between an alien and a test.
Or between a crocodile and my neighbour's dog.
Or between a big, purple, hairy monster and the diving board.
It's not Myg's fault.
Myg is just there to protect me, and sometimes works too hard.

When Myg works too hard, it is up to me to take charge.

If I don't, Myg can get carried away, seeing danger when there is none.

And, when Myg gets carried away, other parts of my brain don't work properly.

My thinking brain switches off.

Because Myg is working too hard, my thinking brain takes a break.

And, when my thinking brain takes a break, I can't think clearly.

So my brilliant brain can't work so brilliantly.

All those brilliant things that my brain can do have to wait until Myg calms down.

My remembering.

My concentrating.

My learning.

22

This is when I have to take charge.

This is when I have to help Myg.

And I start by saying, 'Hey, Myg. I'm OK.

You can relax. I can do this.'

Because sometimes it is OK to feel worried or nervous.
And sometimes I can manage it myself.
I've got lots of ideas which you could use, too ...
just in case you have to take charge of your Myg.
And be a Child in Charge.

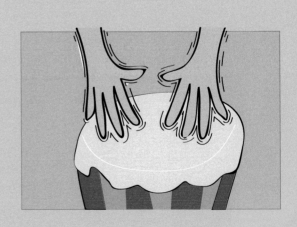

24

I am really good at being a Child in Charge.

But sometimes I need help to be a brilliant
Child in Charge.

So then I ask someone I trust to help me.

If I have a really big worry.
If I am very anxious about something.
If I don't think I can do it myself.
Then it is OK to let that trusted
person take charge for me.

As long as I tell that trusted person what my worry is.

That I am feeling really anxious. That I don't think I can manage what is happening ...

Then, that trusted person will take charge for me.

27

If someone I trust takes charge for me, it means they will help me with my feelings, help me with my anxieties, until I can do it myself.

Until I can be a Child in Charge.

28

And you can be a Child in Charge, too.

Child in Charge

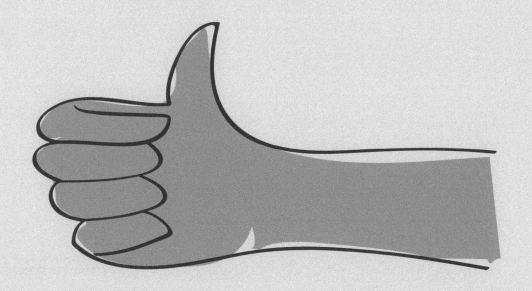